In the

Simplest

Things

In the Simplest Things

MISTY L. BUTLER

Published by Studio of Misty L. Butler

Photography by Misty L. Butler
Edited by Charles Strohmer

Published by Studio of Misty L. Butler

ISBN: 9781097987160

Names in some of the following stories have been changed.

Dedication

I dedicate this book to Megan Davidson, who was a friend to everyone, and a model of service and love in the church and community.

CONTENTS

"All Kinds of Amazing Things"

"Angels?"

My eyes lit up with curiosity as I pedaled the stationary bike at the gym. I had been feeling glum that morning after some long-awaited plans had fallen through, and I wasn't interested in talking with anyone. Now, however, my mood brightened.

"You saw angels?"

Robert, a friendly older man, had begun chatting as soon as he seated himself on the bicycle beside me. I noticed a few details about him right away. Huge scars ran down the side of his right leg until they disappeared behind a knee brace, and he winced in pain as his feet pushed the pedals. But he smiled and laughed too.

A physical therapist walked over and asked Robert how he was doing. "Remember," he said, "our goal is to eventually have you here eight hours at a time, to see if you would be able to tolerate returning to a regular workday." Overhearing that made me more curious about this mysterious man.

After the physical therapist walked off, I said to Robert, "Wow, eight hours? And here I was just hoping to get in forty-five minutes of exercise today!" He laughed and began telling me his story.

"Honey," he said, "I'm working so hard on this rehabilitation so I can go back to work. You see, about a year ago I almost left this earth. Yes, ma'am, I had a horrible accident on the job and almost didn't make it."

"Oh no!" I said, wanting to ask more but trying not to pry. "That's so scary."

"Oh, it was, honey. There I was working in the warehouse on one of those big machines I've used every single day for years. But I had an accident with the machine and became trapped under it. I screamed and cried out for help, but everyone had gone to lunch, so no one heard me. I was pinned under that heavy equipment and my leg and hip were crushed. Honey, I knew it was the end. I wasn't going to make it so I started praying. First I prayed for my grandkids," he said, emotion touching his voice. "I prayed that they would be taken care of and know that their pops loved them. Then I prayed, 'God, if you're ready to take me, I'm ready to go.'"

"What happened then?" I asked, enraptured and hoping to hear more.

"That's when I saw the angels."

"Angels? You saw angels? What did they look like?"

"Oh, honey, they were the most beautiful things! I can't even describe their colors. They were brighter than anything I've ever seen on earth. And there were four of them, flying right in front of me," he said, waving his hand in front of his face. "I just watched those angels and felt ready to leave and go on with them. But then I heard something off in the distance. One of my co-workers was screaming across the warehouse, 'Hold on! I'm coming! I'm coming!'"

I was now so caught up in his story that I didn't even look at the screen on my bike as it flashed my distance and heart rate. I kept my eyes on Robert as he continued. His next memory was of a Life Flight ride on a helicopter, then waking up in a hospital bed days later. A year of surgeries, extensive rehabilitation, and countless days of tears, pain, and depression had begun for him.

I was feeling so sober from his story that I felt foolish for having felt so glum that morning.

As he slowly pedaled he explained that he was undergoing the demanding physical therapy at the gym because he was determined to return to work. The physical therapists were gradually increasing his exercises until he would eventually be there for eight hours a day, to see if he would be able to work a full shift again.

"It's a miracle," I said, shaking my head in awe.

"Oh, honey!" Robert answered kindly and with assurance, "The Lord can do all kinds of amazing things!"

His words really struck me. I had been struggling to believe that God was doing very much in my life, let alone anything amazing. As soon as I got home I sat down at my computer and wrote out Robert's story. I didn't want to forget the simple, hard-working, scarred man who showed up right beside me when I had lost expectations of anything good coming from my circumstances.

Perhaps we can't see angelic wings or "all kinds of amazing things" right now, but we can choose to trust that God is doing them.

Kids' Thoughts on My Teaching Style

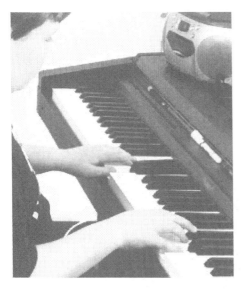

For much of my life, I have been working with kids—volunteering at church, teaching piano, babysitting, or helping them with school work. By interacting with so many different kids, I've learned so much about myself, and that my job might look a bit different from one day to the next.

When you work with young people, you play many roles! I have started my day reminding a student to count out his half notes, listened to my next student vent about his school teacher, and then helped a teenage girl get a wasp out of her car. One of the personal lessons I quickly learned from working with kids is that they are completely, unapologetically, 100 percent honest. Hearing their candid remarks has brought me a lot of surprise and laughter over the years. Based on feedback I've received, most of my students seem to think of me as a "fun" piano teacher. Due to my enthusiastic, motivating manner, however, I wonder if at times I get a bit tougher than I realize. One afternoon a stout young boy with glasses paused in his lesson and asked, "Were you in the army?"

"In the army?" I repeated in confusion.

"Yeah," he nodded. "You're so strict."

Another time, I was excitedly teaching new concepts to a seven-year-old boy, energetically explaining how to add a staccato touch to his song and attempting to push him just a little harder. As his lesson ended I packed up his books and led him out of my studio, with a reminder of how he could excel with a bit of practice. "I just really need to go relax," he said, walking out of my room.

One Friday afternoon a young boy was leaving my studio after I wrote several assignments in his notebook. "I think you can do great on those songs," I called after him. "Try to get a lot of practice and you'll see huge progress. Stick with it! Have a fun weekend!"

With a slight shake of his head, he muttered, "I don't have time for fun."

Another time a freckle-faced little girl entered my studio, sat down at the piano bench, and started hitting the keys mindlessly. Trying to steer her toward focusing, I asked, "Are you ready to get to work?"

"Let's get this party started," she groaned, putting her hands on the keys.

Then there was the Monday afternoon when I opened up a little girl's assignment book. Beside the instructions I'd written for her the previous week, she had added her own entry. At the top of the page she had written "Misty's Orders" and drawn a picture of me with steam coming out of my ears.

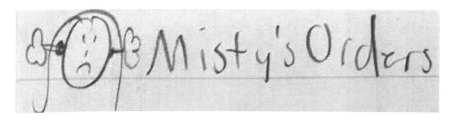

A few slightly tough tendencies? Hey, that's my job, right?

Where You and I Come From

I come from my Father, from hands that raised mountains,
from hands that carved canyons and seas,
from eyes that roamed over the whole earth and saw
this world might need someone like me.

I come from my Maker, who cast stars in heaven,
who numbered each grain of sand,
who breathed dust to life, set worlds in motion,
and made me a part of His plan.

I come from my Friend, who says that He loves me,
in ways that I cannot conceive,
who says He will lead, if I will follow,
who says He will meet all my needs.

In Adoration

When I stop to gaze toward the heavens above,
to the infinite blue in the light of day
or the stars and the moon in darkness so deep,
I'm overwhelmed by Your limitless love.
In adoration, I fall to my knees.

When I stop to remember Your constant care,
Your presence so near in each test and trial,
Your all-seeing eyes never leaving my face,
Your ears ever hearing each breath of prayer,
in adoration, I pause to give praise.

When I stop to breathe in a flower's sweet scent
or smile at the laugh of an innocent child,
or watch You redeem what seemed without hope,
I know I am seeing Your holy handprint.
In adoration, my joy overflows.

When I stop to think of Your only Son
descending to live in such chaos below,
suffering in cruelty, dying in pain
for all God's creation—each lost, lonely one—
in adoration, I give Him my thanks.

Your forgiveness is more than I comprehend.
Your strength is greater than words could express.
Your love reaches deeper than humanity's fall.
Your grace surpasses all of my sins.
So in adoration, I give you my all.

Held in His Arms

Despite a relationship I had that seemed certain to head to the altar, it crashed, along with my dreams. I fell asleep one night the way I had so many other nights during that time, my heart heavy and my mind lamenting the reality of so much disappointment.

Also like many other nights, sorrow crept into my sleep. My dreams took me back to a house where I once lived—a small, country home with slightly slanted walls and sloping floors. In my dream, I was lying on the tile floor facedown and sobbing, "I don't understand why I'm here again. Why am I back in this place? Why does this keep happening?"

Immediately, I felt two strong but tender arms encircle me and pull me into His lap as I wept on the floor. Although I didn't raise my head to see a face, I felt a warmth radiating from His presence and recognized that I was being held in the arms of Jesus. He gently rocked me back and forth as He repeatedly whispered these words, "Shh, I've got you. I've got you."

I awoke and took deep breaths as my eyes struggled to adjust to the darkness of the room. *That was a dream?* I thought in confusion. *But it was so real. I physically felt Him holding me. That couldn't have been a dream.*

As I crawled through the various stages of grief, I clung to the memory of that dream. I still didn't know why my life had taken the paths it had, but Jesus had given me a moment of experiencing His presence so strongly that His touch had seemed tangible.

In the days that followed, when sorrow and confusion swept over me, I remembered the protectiveness of His arms and His whisper that soothed so simply, "I've got you. I've got you."

Some Things Are Best Left a Mystery

Before I taught piano professionally, I worked many jobs—answering phones, filing, punching in data-entry. Honestly, none of those jobs were very interesting or mentally stimulating, until the afternoon the fire alarm went off.

The office where I worked was sectioned off behind glass doors and windows on the second door of a large brick building. My typical day consisted of hours in a cubicle doing data-entry, interrupted by a fifteen-minute break in the morning, a thirty-minute lunch, and another break in the afternoon.

I was in a stall in the upstairs restroom on the afternoon break in question when, without warning, the shrill scream of the fire alarm echoed loudly in the restroom. My heart thumped, and my breathing sped up. *Don't panic,* I inwardly advised myself. *You're not far from the exit. You know what to do. You'll make it. Just get outside!*

I tore out of that stall and raced through the restroom. *But what about my co-workers?* I thought. *Will they make it out? Will everyone be okay?* Then I realized that they were probably evacuating the building right at that moment or even waiting outside for me.

I rushed into the hallway, where the shrieking alarm was even louder. Instead of fleeing down the main stairway that I climbed every morning to the second floor, I took a shortcut toward the stairwell, swung the door open, and took off down the steps, moving as fast as possible without tripping and tumbling.

My colleagues will be so thankful to see I made it out alive! I thought when I reached the bottom of the stairwell. I was panting and frantic, a hundred thoughts racing through my head. No doubt Karen and Teresa, the women who worked in cubicles beside me, and Jeff, my boss, had already made it outside and were frantically looking for me. *I hope they aren't panicking or trying to go back into the burning building to search for me. Surely the fire department won't let them back in! Surely they're all waiting just outside. They'll be so relieved once they see that—*

I pushed open the outer door at the bottom of the stairwell and ran full-force onto the patio where I expected to be met by dozens of employees falling to their knees and shouting with joy at my arrival.

Silence. I stood gasping for breath and glanced around. No one stood on the patio. No firemen were jumping from their fire trucks or spraying the building with water from their heavy hoses. I saw traffic making its way down Scottsville Road and cars lining up at drive-thru windows. It was an ordinary afternoon.

I turned around and looked at the large building. No flames leapt from its walls. No smoke poured from its windows. *What's going on?* I wondered, now feeling a little foolish.

I looked around self-consciously and then walked back up to the second floor as nonchalantly as possible. I entered our office and saw everyone staring intently at their computers, focused on their work. Everyone seemed cool and so together, but I was completely rattled and didn't want to be the young temp who didn't know what was going on. Sitting down in my cubicle I wiped my sweaty forehead and tried to calm my racing heart. I picked up the next paper in my stack and tried to look as if I was focusing on it.

I couldn't concentrate. My thoughts screamed in confusion. *I definitely heard a fire alarm, no question about that. But hadn't anybody else in the building heard it? Did it only go off in the restroom and hallway? Maybe the other employees had been forewarned of it, but nobody thought to tell the lowly temp?*

I was dying to ask my colleagues, but I was still shaking from the adrenaline rush and didn't want to embarrass myself by saying that I'd fled the building in a state of hysteria.

I never discovered the answers to those questions. I decided not to say anything. I was glad that none of my co-workers had witnessed my fiasco because I knew they would have teased me relentlessly for the rest of my employment there.

I decided that some things in life ought to just remain a mystery, to me and to others.

To Just Be Whole

She flashes the brightest, perfect smile
and always wears the latest style.
Her life seems always in control.
You think with longing, "Now she is whole."

His business always seems to thrive,
and only the newest car he drives.
He never fails to reach a goal.
You think with longing, "Now he is whole."

Their house is spotless, built brand new.
Their kids seem so well-mannered too.
Their marriage only seems to grow.
You think with longing, "Now they are whole."

They come to church, dressed to charm,
Bibles tucked beneath their arms,
perfection on their faces glow.
You think with longing, "Oh, to be whole."

But you don't see the hidden tears,
regrets and struggles through the years,
the times they nearly let everything go.
They think with longing, "We are not whole."

You don't see the fights or pain,
the risks that didn't end in gain,
or the hurts their hearts have known.
They ache with longing, "To just be whole."

If you could only see, you'd find
we're all tattered and torn inside.
No matter what façade we show,
only Jesus can make us whole.

Unexpected Peace

Life had been a definite struggle lately, so I could have easily justified an extra hour or two of sleep. But my alarm wouldn't allow it. Beeping me awake early one Saturday morning, I blearily remembered volunteering to help with the community meal delivery program.

An hour later, our van loaded with bags and boxes of food, two other volunteers and I began navigating the town, knocking on doors, cheerfully greeting each person who answered. Some were talkative; others mumbled "thank you" with sadness in their eyes, reminding me that everyone carries sorrow we know nothing about.

After completing our deliveries I returned to my car in the church parking lot. Not in a hurry to leave, I walked around to the front of the church and curiously eyed the historic edifice, wondering if its doors might be unlocked. When I saw a priest push the main wooden door open, I swiftly followed him.

I put my weight against the heavy door, pushed, and walked inside, where silence and beauty hushed my every distraction. I walked slowly and silently through the sanctuary, taking in the breathtaking artistry and ornate depictions of Jesus and His saints. Candles flickered. Sunlight glittered through stained glass windows. Angelic figures guarded the altar. This was the first time I'd wandered into this beautiful place of worship here in my own town. As I sat quietly in a wooden pew, a peace I hadn't felt in a while washed over me.

That visit led to others. I returned to the sanctuary whenever my heart felt heavy. Now I often stop and enter through those large wooden doors each week to pause from life's chaos and find a glimmer of hope.

I know that God is present in my piano studio or my simple home, but I have learned that certain places speak to our souls and reveal God's presence in ways we fail to recognize elsewhere. In moments when I feel alone, I remind myself that God is always as close as I know Him to be when I sit on the wooden pews of that ornate house of worship.

Kids' Thoughts on Song Requests

I try to incorporate a wide variety of songs into my students' repertoire. Despite all the fundamentals I want my students to learn, I also want them to also have songs to play simply because they enjoy them. Little girls often request to learn songs by a recent popular artist, such as Taylor Swift, while teenage girls gravitate toward songs by Lorde. One talented young boy, using only his ear and no sheet music, learns every single song from the Mario Brothers video games. He can play each one, complete with sound effects, and tell you what happens in the game when that particular song is played.

Sometimes a student suggests a song that leaves me laughing. A rowdy second-grade boy looked at me in exasperation one day and asked, "Are there any wrestling songs I can play on the piano?"

I also have young kids hear a song and mistake it for something else. A nine-year-old boy once walked through the door of my studio as I was playing "Great Is Thy Faithfulness."

"What's the name of that song?" he asked.

"Great is Thy Faithfulness," I answered. "Our church band will be playing it this Sunday."

"Great is Thy Faithfulness?" he asked in confusion. "I thought for sure that was 'When Pigs Fly'!"

Occasionally, little girls deviate from their typical song requests and ask me for something I'm not expecting. To a tiny, blond second-grade girl, I excitedly said, "We're about to start practicing Christmas music! Do you like Christmas music?"

"Yes," she answered calmly, "but I like 'Born in the U.S.A.' better."

And there was the dainty girl with brown curls. "What's one song you'd really like to learn?" I asked.

Without any hesitation, she answered, "We Will Rock You."

She wasn't the first to request that song. So guess what has become a favorite among my students?

And, yes, the girls play it too.

On Sorrowful, Silent Saturdays

"For we are buried together with Him by baptism into death; that as Christ is risen from the dead by the glory of the Father, so we also may walk in newness of life." ~ Romans 6:4 (DRA)

When Jesus hung on the cross on that Friday long ago, dying, the agony and heartbreak of His disciples must have been unimaginable. Yet I always wonder if the next day—that sorrowful, silent Saturday—was even worse. Perhaps on Friday His followers were in denial and disbelief, too shocked to process what was happening to their Messiah, the one who was supposed to rescue them. Perhaps pieces of their hearts still hoped He would miraculously come down from that cross and conquer the Romans once and for all.

But what about that next day, when they could not look upon Jesus' face or hear His voice? Imagine the finality, anguish, and hopelessness when the disciples realized their friend was truly gone. Today we spend the Saturday before Easter knowing that resurrection Sunday is just hours away. The disciples spent Saturday believing that all the hope they had clung to was now dead and buried. But on resurrection Sunday God brought deep rejoicing to those same disciples.

My prayers and hopes are that our own sorrowful, silent Saturdays— those times of confusion, waiting, and anguish—will be preludes to resurrection Sundays, when God will take what appears dead and hopeless and command it to rise into unstoppable life.

"Jesus said to her: 'I am the resurrection and the life: he that believeth in me, although he be dead, shall live.'" John 11:25 (DRA)

Bread of Angels

"Then the Lord said to Moses, 'I am going to rain down bread from heaven for you.'" ~ Exodus 16:4 (NET)

"In the evening the quail came up and covered the camp, and in the morning a layer of dew was all around the camp. When the layer of dew had evaporated, there on the surface of the desert was a thin flaky substance, thin like frost on the earth. When the Israelites saw it, they said to one another, 'What is it?' because they did not know what it was. Moses said to them, 'It is the bread that the Lord has given you for food.'" ~ Exodus 16:13-15 (NET)

As the Israelites journeyed through what seemed like a never-ending desert, they were misled by something all of us fall prey to at times: they were deceived by their emotions.

Our feelings can tell us that our circumstances are hopeless, with no chance of improving. Intense emotions can cloud our perception until we lose all expectations of joy in our future. It's an age-old deception, even for believers in God.

After Moses led the Israelites out of slavery, they spent forty years wandering through the desert. In Egypt, under cruel rulers, they had been inhumanely overworked and beaten mercilessly. Yet even though it was God Himself who had set them free, a change took place in their emotions.

As the Israelites' time in the desert stretched on, their initial rejoicing over their newfound freedom diminished into frustration, fear, and despondency because they hadn't yet reached the Promised Land. They whined and complained to Moses. They regretted leaving the life they'd known, despite how grueling and miserable it had been. They predicted that starvation and death awaited them. They even lamented the fact that they were alive. The Israelites had become convinced that every distressing emotion they felt was, indeed, fact.

But their emotions were lying to them. Their future was not going to be bleak. Starvation was not their destiny. God sent down manna from heaven. The very people who were certain of starving ate the bread of angels.

Emotions can be deceiving. It's easy for us to wail that we were better off trapped in old circumstances. When we feel doomed to a hopeless, desolate fate, that might not be an accurate depiction of what awaits. God might be sending us the bread of angels.

Kids' Thoughts on Their Parents

I wonder if my students' parents realize some of the comments I hear about dear old mom and dad.

*A blond pre-teen entered my studio one afternoon with an appalled expression on her face. "My dad is learning to play guitar," she announced in disbelief.

"That's awesome!" I said. At her eye roll, I continued, "Do you think your dad shouldn't be learning to play guitar?"

"No!" she exclaimed in horror, "he's FIFTY!"

"Do you think fifty-year-olds shouldn't learn to play guitar?" I asked. "Adults can learn new skills too!"

"But he's BALD!"

*I once taught a teenage girl whose playing exhibited such talent and artistry that I asked, "Are your parents musical?"

"Not really," she answered with a shake of her head, then asked, "Do you know who the band Maroon 5 is?" At my nod, she continued, "My dad goes through the house pretending he's Adam Levine—but it's just not working."

*An eight-year-old girl entered her lesson and announced proudly, "My dad has been helping me with the C chord."

"He has?" I asked. "I didn't know your dad played piano?"

"Well, he doesn't play piano," she explained, "but he knows chords—I think because he's a banker." That seemed to make perfect sense to her, but definitely not to me.

* A young boy wasn't at all happy with his mom's rule that each child must take at least three years of piano lessons. "Sometimes my lessons seem so long, I feel like I'm stuck in music hell," he commented as he gathered up his books and left my studio.

Called by Name

I sat at attention behind the piano in the campus dance studio where I worked part-time accompanying ballet classes. I never could relax in this job. It wasn't like many previous jobs, where I would gather with co-workers in the break room to chat about the weekend or laugh at their jokes. Instead, the dance professor and I would greet each other daily with a formal, "Good morning," and then an intense ninety-minute dance class would begin, which required my undivided attention.

Afterward, the students would file out and I would lock my music books in the cabinet, place the piano bench on top of the upright piano, roll it against the wall, and then walk a mile back to where I had parked my car on a side street downtown.

This dance professor was all business. He always directed the class at a fast pace and dictated instructions through a heavy accent that demanded my non-stop focus to pick up on my cues to start playing. After demonstrating each exercise to the students, the professor would look at me with a strike of his hand in the air and call out in a strong voice, "Maestro!"

And with his four-count preparation, I would begin the music.

Sometimes after giving me my cue, he would see that the students needed additional instructions, so my hands would wait quietly on the keys until he continued, "Fifth Position! And!" The heavily accented "and" was my cue to start the music. Week after week, along with observing the meter and tempo he demonstrated, I would stay alert for "Maestro!" or "And!"

But one day, he slipped from his usual formal demeanor.

In the tired voice of a weary professor he looked at me and said quietly, "An adagio, please, Misty."

His personal request caught me off guard. It was a huge contrast in a formal environment where I felt I operated mechanically and was unsure if the instructor or students even knew my name. My ears perked up at the sound of my name. I no longer felt like a piece of gear in some machinery.

From that simple act of human kindness, I sensed the longing that God has planted in each of us to be known by name.

To the weeping woman at the vacant tomb, Jesus spoke her name: Mary. To the hemorrhaging woman grasping for the edge of his clothing, Jesus spoke the familial title: Daughter. To a paralyzed man lying on a mat, Jesus said: Son.

Calling us by name or by an affectionate title, God singles us out in His welcoming grace. He recognizes each of us as an individual that He knows personally. We are not cogs in a machine. God invites each of us to know Him, not as a distant, unknown God, but as the Father we know personally, by name.

"Fear not, for I have redeemed you; I have called you by name, you are mine." ~ Isaiah 43:1 (TLB)

When Cloudy Days Are Beautiful

Some mornings invite me to hear in the hush what can't be heard in the rush. One of those mornings the cool air through my open window caused me to snuggle a little deeper under my blankets, and the overcast sky seemed to whisper, "Don't hurry."

Instead of rushing into my day, I sat at my computer to unravel my thoughts. A breeze lightly fluttered my white lace curtains. The sound of children laughing in the nearby schoolyard coaxed me outside. I smiled as I walked by their energetic game of kickball. Their excitement had escalated as the school year neared its end. A few miles away, the bells from the campus tower chimed their familiar tune. A train whistled as it rolled through town.

How often do I notice these sounds?

I walked through the neighborhood of cozy, older homes and stopped to admire a manicured lawn, splashed with red, purple, and yellow thriving flowers. Farther on, I saw piles of fresh lumber where the foundation for a new home had already been poured.

How often do I notice these sights?

I walked past a neighbor who was out mowing his yard. The fragrance of freshly cut grass filled the air. I smiled as I breathed in its sweetness.

How often do I notice these scents?

Some days beckon me to slow down, be quiet, to stop, look, and listen. Fresh wooden boards, colorful flowers, the laughter of children, sweet smell of grass, train whistles traveling to unknown destinations—those aren't unique to unrushed days or cloudy mornings. They are ordinary gifts that are usually present in our daily rush of work, of errands, of the chaos to get things done.

We simply must choose to get quiet enough to enjoy them.

"Play Good"

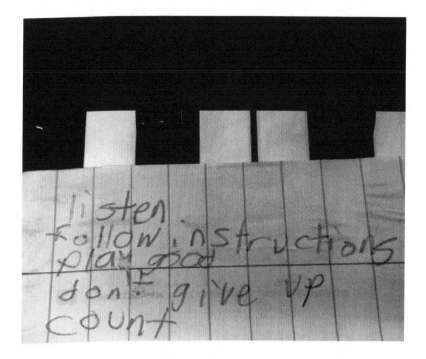

At different points throughout the year, I ask my students to write down goals to work on to improve their playing. Often these goals are specific to whatever a student is struggling with—connect slurs, observe rests, use correct fingers on scales.

One student's list of five goals really caught my attention: Listen, follow instructions, play good, don't give up, count. Although he chose these goals based on how he could improve his musicianship, I saw how they could be expanded to apply to our lives as a whole.

Listen. Listen to the people in our lives who offer wise words when our thoughts blind us from clarity. Listen to the words of encouragement and hope that we often dismiss. Listen for those still whispers of the Holy Spirit guiding us in the details of our lives.

Follow instructions. "Jesus said . . . 'You shall love the Lord your God with all your heart, with all your soul, and with all your mind.' This is the first and great commandment. And the second is like it, 'You shall love your neighbor as yourself.'" ~ Matthew 22:37-39 (NKJV)

Play good. Life is full of stress, chaos, and work. We easily find ourselves overwhelmed by constant pressures. Pause to remember what makes you smile. Laugh with others, observe the growth of a flower, run through the rain, find little details to celebrate. Remember that the simplest things are often the best things. "Play good."

Don't give up. You'll want to. Circumstances will leave you discouraged and convinced you can't finish. Your dreams might move slower than you had imagined. You might make countless attempts at the same goal but still seem to fail. Still, don't give up.

Count. Count as valuable, cherished time the moments you are with people you care about. Count each sunset as a daily benediction and your every birthday as a celebration of another year on earth. Count even the smallest gifts as blessings—the scent of flowers, the sight of clouds, the taste of your favorite dish, the furry softness of a pet, the sound of your favorite song.

Life isn't always easy, but so many simple joys await our notice. So listen, follow instructions, play good, don't give up, and count.

A Song in the Salon

I stood in the hair salon talking with a few people. One stylist chatted as she trimmed an older lady's hair, while another stylist, Debbie, rinsed her client's hair in a large sink.

I taught piano next door to the salon, and the conversation turned to music. "Oh, you're a musician?" Debbie said. "Have you heard Patricia sing?" she asked, motioning to her client, whose hair she was still rinsing. "She has the most beautiful voice! Patricia, sing something for Misty! Let her hear you sing!"

Patricia shook her head in embarrassed laughter, "No, no," she said. But Debbie, along with Patricia's husband who stood nearby, chimed in, "Oh, sing, Patricia! You have a beautiful voice. Sing something for us!"

Realizing their prodding wasn't going to stop, Patricia finally gave in. Now seated in a stylist's chair with a towel wrapped around her head and a wet curl dripping water down her face, she closed her eyes thoughtfully. The room waited in silence, and then Patricia's deep, soulful voice began an old tune I recognized as "Peaceful in the Arms of My Lord":

"This old world is full of pain and misery.
Sometimes Satan stands and lashes out at me.
But with Jesus on my side, I am satisfied,
and it's so peaceful in the arms of my Lord.
It's so peaceful in the arms of my Lord.
In His presence, I am sheltered from the storm.
It's so good to have His spirit.
It's so good to have His word,
and it's so peaceful in the arms of my Lord."

Debbie stood with her hands clasped in front of her face, tears forming in her eyes. Patricia's husband's eyes sparkled with pride, and the others in the salon sighed at the beauty of the moment.

I stood thoughtfully and considered how I had just observed a simple act of pure worship—an act that we often relegate to Sunday mornings or requiring a pastor or priest. But worship occurs any time we choose to honor our Savior. And we can honor Him in our day-to-day lives, as we earn our paychecks, fold laundry, clean the baby, or greet the cashier at the convenience store—in the simplest times and simplest places.

A message, a prayer, or a song delivered before an audience of thousands isn't worth more than the humble strains sung from the lips of a weary, wet-haired woman inside the walls of a beauty parlor.

In Your Hands

In your hands, water becomes wine,
leprous skin is cleansed,
blind eyes see the sun.

In your hands, deaf ears hear a melody,
lame legs dance for joy,
morsels make a meal.

In your hands, angry waves turn calm,
death gives way to life,
demons run and hide.

Not only then but still today,
Your hands gently care
for everything placed in them.

In your hands, broken wounds are bound,
painful hurts are soothed,
broken hearts are healed.

In your hands, confusion falls away,
Your spirit floods our souls,
the pathway becomes clear.

In your hands, weakness turns to strength,
loss turns into gain,
life becomes brand new.

Creating a Fashion Trend

I dressed carefully for the Good Friday service on that April evening in my early twenties. I slipped into a lightweight top, dressy pants, and a brand new pair of white and gold sandals, my toenails perfectly painted. Later that night it was supposed to turn cool, so I grabbed a light jacket as I headed to my car.I have always loved the Easter season and the earth's transition into spring. So I was sure that this was going to be a good night.

The words, music, and entire Good Friday service were beautiful. As the service ended, I tucked the meaning of this special weekend inside me as I walked with my boyfriend out of the church. Struck by the sudden drop in temperature, I gasped as the cold took my breath away. Suddenly, my light springy outfit and dainty sandals seemed ridiculous. I should have dressed for Christmas.

Arriving at Daniel's house I burrowed my feet under a cushion of his couch and asked, "Do you have any s-s-socks I can borrow?" A minute later he tossed me a pair of Nike socks, and I laughed when I pulled them over my icy toes. They looked so huge on my miniature feet. But I thankfully pulled them over my icy toes as he said, "I'm hungry. I haven't had any supper. Have you?"

"No, and I'm hungry too, but where can we go?" My mind ran through the restaurant options in my small hometown.

He suggested going to the Flavor Isle, an old-fashioned burger and ice cream joint with the walk-up outdoor window for placing carry-out orders. I quickly agreed, my stomach growling louder at the thought of delicious mini-cheeseburgers and fries.

As we bundled ourselves up in jackets, I felt too cold to take off the comfy socks. So I did the practical thing—I shoved my socked feet into the sandals to keep them warm. "Do you mind walking up to the window and ordering our food?" I asked. "That way no one else will see me in these socks and sandals." That's how it worked at the Flavor Isle. Customers walked up to the outside window to place their order, then drove around town to kill time as their food was cooking—one of those little perks of small-town life. He laughed at the heels of the bulky men's socks hanging out under the back strap of my sandals.

We drove down Main Street in the dark, quiet town and quickly approached our destination.

"Hey, there are no lights on," he observed. "I think they're closed."

"Aw, closed!" I pouted in disappointment, glancing at the clock. Sure enough, the little burger and ice cream joint was pitch black and locked up. We'd be having no mini-burgers or milkshakes that night.

"Where else can we go?" I wondered out loud and rubbed my growling stomach. We drove down the street, crossed the railroad tracks, and debated our limited options.

"Hey, how about Donita's Diner?" he suggested. "We could relax and eat inside."

"Yeah," I agreed as my mouth began watering at the thought of fried country food just inside the doors of the casual diner.

We walked inside the crowded restaurant and were immediately greeted with several warm waves and calls of, "Hey, come sit with us," as other members of the church had also decided to enjoy a late supper. I waved excitedly back at them and began walking across the floor when,
"Oh NO!" I groaned in horror under my breath, as I walked across the crowded diner with its bright lights shining down on me.

"I forgot about the socks!" I whisper-screamed to Daniel as I walked in embarrassment toward the table. The socks' heels gaped out from my sandals and dragged the floor while the toes scrunched up under my toe straps.

How do I get out of a situation like this? I thought. I could go to the bathroom and take the socks off, but that would require more walking in front of everyone in the restaurant, and I was already mortified. I slid hurriedly down into the chair awaiting me and whispered to the woman sitting beside me, "Cindy, I feel like such a dork. My feet were cold, so I put on his socks and forgot to take them off before I came in." Her eyes immediately glanced to my feet with the baggy men's socks scrunched under my beautiful sandals just below my neatly-pressed dress pants, and she burst out laughing—laughing 'til she almost cried.

Trying to appear unaffected, I reached under the table, felt for a foot, and tried to appear cool and indifferent as I discreetly slipped off my sandals and removed the humongous male socks while people all around me sat eating their dinners. They had probably seen people take their shoes and socks off under the tables in restaurants all the time, right? I stuffed the embarrassing socks inside my purse and tried to pretend the eyes and amused nearby glances had nothing to do with me.

Remember the fashion phase that began several years ago when some men started wearing socks with sandals? I bet I started that. Those men in the diner who were checking out my feet may have gotten some ideas.

That was one spring look I'll remember forever. Although I look back on that memory with laughter now, I definitely don't want to make such drastic fashion blunders a habit.

In Broken Places

Each Lenten season the word "brokenness" replays in my mind.

As the people of a broken world determined to crush Jesus, the one who came to save them, Jesus' final days on earth were filled with brokenness.

At the disciples' last supper with Jesus, bread was broken. On the cross where Jesus died for us, our Lord's body was broken. At Jesus' last breath, the earth shook and the veil of the temple was torn in two.

Today is not so different. We hear of brokenness in faraway places. We experience it in our own lives. Each one of us has distinct memories of times when our hearts felt too broken to be mended.

But the fasting, waiting, or preparation during Lent moves us toward a day of celebration, a day when a sealed tomb opened and Jesus walked out alive. His passage from a dark, somber grave into perfect, everlasting light brings hope that the darkest places in our lives can become places of overflowing light.

Each night as I sleep and the dark hours slip toward dawn, a soft light gradually reaches through my bedroom window. The glass panes are covered with closed blinds and heavy curtains, yet the morning light still finds a slight crack at the edge of the curtains and breaks in, rousing me from darkness.

"In him was life; and the life was the light of men. And the light shineth in darkness; and the darkness comprehended it not." ~ John 1:4-5 (KJV)

Kids' Thoughts on Me

I hear so many funny or brutally honest comments from my students that I'm often surprised when they simply say something sweet. A round, lovable young boy asked me one day, "How have you not gotten married yet? They should be lining up!"

Often, however, they can be pretty blunt and funny at the same time. I remember the time one young girl questioned my penchant for neatness and order, wondering if it was more like a mental illness.

"Oh, don't touch that!" I said as she tampered with the poster hanging above the piano. "It'll get crooked."

She turned to me wide-eyed and asked, "Do you have C.O.D.?"

"C.O.D.?" I asked, confused.

"You know, where you're real picky about having everything in perfect order and in just the right spot?"

One night I sat by the piano tiredly and greeted my last student of the day, a giggly, bright-eyed girl who was always overflowing with energy. "So what do you do for work? Like, for a job?" she asked.

Not only are some students unsure of my career, they are also unsure of my size.

"What did you do for your birthday?" I asked a little girl who just turned nine years old.

"We went to Jump Air Zone," she answered.

"Jump Air Zone? And you didn't invite me?" I teased.

"Well, how much do you weigh?" her brother piped in. "Because there's a weight limit of 300."

I have spent quite a bit of time baby-sitting throughout the years. One bright day in early spring I played basketball with a boy who was in late elementary school. "Hey, your throwing has gotten really good!" I said, as he threw the ball to me.

"Your shooting is terrible," he replied.

Basketball is not the only thing I've been told is not a strength of mine.

One October evening as a freckle-faced girl finished playing "O Christmas Tree," I exclaimed cheerfully, "Your song is putting me in the Christmas spirit!"

"I know, me too!" she said. "I've already knitted and crocheted some Christmas presents!"

"You knit and crochet?" I asked, impressed. "I don't know how to do either. Now, did you have any questions on that song? You were looking at the page like you were wondering something."

"No, I was just looking at it so I could think ahead, like in chess."

"Oh, you play chess? I've never learned how to play chess."

"Well," she said, "it sounds like there's a lot of things you don't know how to do, if you don't mind my saying so."

Later, after trying unsuccessfully to encourage a thirteen-year-old girl to practice, I teased, "If I can't tell you've worked on these songs by next week, I'll be really angry."

"No, you won't," she argued. "You're a nice piano teacher and a church piano player. Church piano players don't get mean and angry."

"Who says church piano players don't get mean and angry?"

"They don't," she insisted. "Drummers are the mean ones. They come to church to beat on things."

My accent can be a source of amusement to my students. "Play me an E on the piano," I instructed a cute little boy who had a pretty strong country accent himself.

"You said Eeeee," he said, looking at me as if I should correct myself.

"That's right," I answered. "Show me where it is on the piano."

He shook his head. Holding his fingers to his lips, he said, "It's pronounced like this: 'E.'"

One night I baby-sat a cute, blue-eyed girl who was in town from St. Louis. I chatted with her quietly as I helped her brush her teeth. After spitting out her toothpaste, she blurted, "You sound like a cowgirl!"

54

Who Do You Say I Am

"When Jesus came to Caesarea Philippi, He asked his disciples, 'Who are the people saying I am?'

'Well,' they replied, 'some say John the Baptist; some, Elijah; some, Jeremiah or one of the other prophets.'

Then He asked them, 'Who do you think I am?'

Simon Peter answered, 'The Christ, the Messiah, the Son of the living God.'"~ Matthew 16:13-16 (TLB)

When Jesus asked His disciples who the people thought He was, they supplied Him with a number of answers. But Jesus didn't stop the conversation there. More pointedly, He asked, "But who do YOU say I am?" Peter spoke up without hesitation, "You are the Christ, Son of the Living God."

That passage reminds us that Jesus asks each of us that same question and waits for each of us to answer. Jesus' question was an invitation, an opportunity for His first-century followers to assert who they truly believed Him to be.

Today, however, we often make ourselves the subject of the question. "Who do people say I am? Do they think I'm attractive or unappealing? Proficient or inept? What's my reputation?" We often ask this question out of a desperation for others' approval. Instead, we could turn this question toward the One who knows all things.

When we are ridiculed, belittled, or don't fit in: "Jesus, who do You say I am?"

When we feel discouraged with ourselves and our circumstances: "Jesus, who do You say I am?"

When we struggle with shame or stigma from addiction, mental illness, or a sin that has gone public: "Jesus, who do You say I am?"

Jesus gives us opportunities to decide who He is. But He also stands ready to answer our questions about who we truly are, no matter what the world might think of us.

"But to all who did receive Him, who believe in His name, He gave the right to become children of God." ~ John 1:12 (ESV)

Prayers of Humble Hearts

"What made you think of asking me?" I said.

As a musician, I am often asked to play or sing for various events in the community, including worship services. This time, however, the organizer for a worship event where I would be leading music asked if I would lead a special prayer. Although I've grown comfortable with public speaking and enjoy interacting with audiences, those tasks typically go to people with louder, more dominant personalities. So out of curiosity, I had asked why she was asking *me* to lead one of the main prayers.

"You have one of the purest hearts," she said. "If your prayers don't knock on the gates of heaven, then there isn't hope for me."

Her words silenced my mind. She hadn't answered, "Because I know you're used to performing in public, hosting recitals, or leading worship." She hadn't said, "Because I know how much time and effort you put into all you do." She had not evaluated my skills or assessed my abilities—just a simple comment on her perception of my heart. I had never thought of my heart as any purer than any one else's, and I had never considered myself to have any special gift or effectiveness toward prayer.

Many of us have heard that "praying is the most powerful thing we can do," yet we don't always operate with that attitude. Plenty of times, we try everything possible to "fix" the situation and then add on some prayers, hoping they'll supplement our results.

How would our lives be different if we believed that our prayers rattled heaven's gates and caused clouds to thunder at the Lord's swift response? How much more peace would we have if we breathed "Amen" with a certainty that dynamic heavenly beings were en route to our situation?

Maybe someday we'll be shown everything that has happened as a result of our prayers. In the meantime, even amid daily concerns that bring weariness or discouragement, we can remind ourselves that prayers aren't measly hopes that God will sprinkle some leftover help in our direction. Our prayers alter the course of history.

A Night Out in My PJs

I walked into my cozy house one evening in early December. It started out as a perfect night. The lights of my Christmas tree were twinkling in my small living room. I turned on some Christmas music and began wrapping Christmas presents. And I was hungry. Never mind that it was 9:30. The Christmas spirit had me feeling pretty sprightly, so I decided to fix a late-night meal of scrambled eggs and toast.

Cheerfully cooking to the sounds of Bing Crosby and Perry Como, I was suddenly startled by loud beeping. "No problem," I told myself. "It's the smoke alarm." It frequently went off when I cooked. But when I checked, it was silent. I followed the sound, and then panicked.

"It's the carbon monoxide detector," I told myself. "It's a leak. I have a leak! Move to fresh air!" Grabbing my cell phone I flung open the back door, rushed out onto my deck, and gulped breaths of cold air. Shaking, I dialed my mom's number.

"You can't stay there!" my mom wailed. "You've got to get out! Call your friends and find a place to stay. Hurry! I'll call you back in a few minutes!"

The beeping was really annoying, and my heart was pounding. I texted a family from church, and they urged me to stay with them. Keeping my back door open to circulate some fresh air, I threw overnight items into a bag, unplugged the carbon monoxide detector, and walked out to the driveway with a coat wrapped around my pajamas.

I was surprised that my mom hadn't called back yet, since she tends to be a worrier in even less urgent circumstances. Sitting in my car and trying to calm down, I dialed my mom's number. She answered immediately with panic in her voice. "Misty! We've been calling and calling, and you didn't answer."

"What?" I responded. My cell phone had never rung or shown any missed calls.

"We were so worried about you. So we called the police. They should be on their way!"

"The police! The police are coming?" Of all times, *now* is when my cell phone malfunctions and doesn't ring in my mom's calls!

I saw a cop car coming down the road and groaned, "I'll call you back, mom. They're here."

I can't believe this, I thought. *Here comes a policeman to my house while I stand in my driveway in reindeer pajamas under an old coat, with colorful footies and slippers. Wait! Have I already put in the bite guard I wear at night?"* I quickly turned my head, pulled out the disgusting mouthpiece and shoved it into my coat pocket. *Great. Now watch the cop be cute.*

He was.

"Your mom's awfully worried about you," the clean-cut officer said after greeting me and confirming my safety.

"I know," I said quickly, and then relayed my story. He was very polite and advised me to call the fire department the next day so they could determine where the leak was coming from. I drove to Jennifer's house, hoping to end the chaotic night with some refreshing sleep. But there was more to come.

My sweet friends, Jennifer and her parents, greeted me warmly and showed me to their couch, which they had cozily made up with a pillow and blankets. The room was warm and comfortable. But after I settled under the blankets, I was too wound up to relax. My mind was racing.

The oven. Oh no.

While scrambling my eggs, I had also pre-heated the oven for some hash browns. Did I turn it off? Did I take out the hash browns? I couldn't remember. I knew I wouldn't sleep a wink until I knew for sure, so I went to Jennifer's room and whispered that I would be back soon.

It was now past midnight as I drove through the quiet streets, and then entered my darkened, toxic house. My oven was fine. Somehow I'd remembered to turn it off in all the commotion.

I drove back to Jennifer's house longing for sleep, knowing tomorrow would be a long day, and I had to get up bright and early for work. As I pulled into the driveway I saw the back door being closed. *That must be the door they wanted me to use,* I concluded. I rushed through the cold air, pushed open that back door, and walked straight into Jennifer's parents' bedroom, instead of coming into the living area like I was expecting. "Oh, sorry!" I said in the quiet.

"It's okay," Jennifer's mom whispered. "I had just let Derby outside."

Trying to scurry from their room, I walked through the darkness, pushed open the next door, and found myself in their bathroom.

Disoriented, I tried the next door, certain that would take me to the hall, but instead I stepped into the bedroom closet.

"Misty, Misty," Jennifer's mom said, opening the door into the hall.

The next day my less than 1,000-square foot house was brimming over with firemen.

Hmm, I thought. *First a cop and now a bevy of firemen. Never had this many men in my house before, that's for sure!* After all, why not look on the bright side.

That began a long, seventeen-day wait for the company to replace my entire heating unit. I spent the next two-and-a-half weeks sleeping at friends' houses, the church's youth house, and even under one of the grand pianos in the old music store where I worked. Of course, knowing I'd be sleeping in the ancient music store, my co-workers made sure to tell me stories about the historic building being haunted.

No ghosts disturbed me, but I was so glad to return to my cozy house and my own bed after two stressful weeks. It all seems pretty funny now. Maybe someday I'll go ask that cute policeman how many other girls he's rescued in their pjs.

The Wait before Bethlehem

A star burned too radiantly for the Wise Men to ignore. Singing angels swept into the sleepy shepherds' night shift. Mary broke into labor, frantic for a place—any place—to give birth.

The course of history was suddenly altered. Lives were abruptly transformed. Earth was touched by a miracle in the blink of an eye.

The events of that Bethlehem night can sound sudden and dramatic— the strange star, an ill-timed delivery, unsuspecting shepherds. But Mary had been feeling the strains of pregnancy for several months. The Wise Men's journey was not a quick overnight getaway.

The earthly arrival of Jesus was not an afterthought. During what must have seemed like endless silence, God had been at work orchestrating the details of mankind's redemption. Prophets had anticipated

Emmanuel's arrival hundreds of years before his birth. Generation after generation of ordinary people, struggling under the pressures of daily life, longed for a Messiah.

When our lives are routine and mundane, with no signs of Christmas bursting into our circumstances, we can remember that we are in the same place as the shepherds before angels appeared in the darkness. We can remember that we are in the same place as the Wise Men before a gleaming star guided them in the right direction.

The night before Jesus' birth most likely gave no clue to most people that a miracle was about to arrive. Like much of our lives, it probably seemed like just another night to them.

But God can show up even in the simplest, most ordinary moments.

Cling to Me

Cling to me, the storm won't last,
though dark clouds linger low,
though waves rise high, fierce and fast,
and winds rage with an angry blast
that seem to always blow.
But cling to me, the storm won't last.

Treetops rage in vengeful dance
as floods consume the budding ground.
Rainfall drowns each flowering plant,
and streaks of blazing lightning flash
as nature strikes with violent sound.
But cling to me, the storm won't last.

The days of sunshine all seem past.
No light shines from the sun or moon.
Though peace seems void on earth so vast,
hold on, stand close, remain steadfast.
The winds and waves will be calm soon.
Just cling to me. The storm won't last.

"You know when I sit down or stand up. You know my thoughts even when I'm far away. You see me when I travel and when I rest at home. You know everything I do." ~ Psalm 139:3 (NLT)

"You keep track of all my sorrows. You have collected all my tears in your bottle. You have recorded each one in your book." ~ Psalm 56:8 (NLT)

We all run into friends whose mood you can gauge as soon as you begin interacting. A distracted look in their eyes, a flattened tone of voice, or a clipped response—these and many other things may reveal that a friend is hurting, upset, or preoccupied.

Many of us believe that God knows our thoughts in the omniscient way that God knows everything, but we sometimes struggle to grasp that

God knows us as a friend knows a friend. He sees the tears we choke back as we try to appear strong. He hears the disguised pain in our voice as we feign a smile and say, "I'm fine." He recognizes the rough parts of our past that keep showing up in our present, and He is aware of our longings for a better future. But even more than that, this friend collects our tears in His bottle.

In fact, I am certain that God knows us even better than our closest friends do. There is no friend like Him..

"I no longer call you slaves, because a master doesn't confide in His slaves. Now you are my friends, since I have told you everything the Father told me." ~ John 15:15 (NLT)

The Pageant Imposter

I had just finished my last set of tricep dips at the gym when an older man I didn't recognize walked by on his way to the locker room. He was wearing a work shirt with a company logo, and I saw his name tag, *Billy*. "Hey, I heard about you trying out for that Miss America pageant!" he called out to me.

I laughed as I pictured myself tripping on the runway in a long evening gown or bumbling over words in an interview competition. Convinced Billy was joking, I teased back, "Yeah! How did you know?"

"Well, it's all over the internet!" he said. Then as he passed another gym member he pointed toward me and said loudly, "Did you hear that she's gonna be in the Miss America pageant?"

Uh-oh. This Billy guy is serious, I thought. For some absurd reason, he thought I was going to be competing in a national pageant, and he wanted all the sweaty exercisers to know that a celebrity was in their midst. What a laugh! How could anyone here in the gym possibly believe this guy. Besides, some of them knew that I was well beyond the age of pageant contestants and that I spend most of my time teaching kids or practicing music.

But Billy kept it up, pointing in my direction while talking animatedly to a man at the leg press. I lowered my head in embarrassment, hating the fact that I was suddenly the center of attention with my messy ponytail and casual gym clothes. Plus, I obviously wasn't competing in any pageants and I hadn't realized that Billy was so serious about it. Suddenly I felt like a fraud—a pageant queen imposter. I skipped the rest of my workout and left the building before I got anymore questions about this pageant.

While driving home, I remembered that a local girl had just made headlines for an upcoming national pageant she'd be competing in. She was a brunette piano player, like me. Although that was all we had in common, I concluded that Billy had mistaken me for her. "Well, I guess I better work on walking more gracefully in heels!" I joked as I retold that story to friends. But then a thought occurred to me, and it changed my attitude toward the case of mistaken identity. It boosted my confidence in a good way.

Most of us see ourselves as simple, ordinary people and we may feel like frauds or imposters if others think highly of us. We look at ourselves and see a pageant imposter while someone else sees a queen. We look at ourselves and see an ordinary handyman, factory worker, or custodian while others see a hard worker with leadership qualities. We look at ourselves and see an average daycare worker, mom, nurse—or piano teacher—while others see a life-changer.

We may not grace a stage, win a contest, or gain the applause of an audience, but someone might be looking up to us in admiration for the beauty, gifts, and joy we bring to the world.

Kids' Thoughts on Love

*"I'm going to be too tall," an eleven-year-old girl moaned at her lesson one day. "I'm already five-feet-two-and-a-half. That's a little taller than you, and I'm just in fifth grade!"

"Being tall is a good thing!" I said, hoping to encourage her. "What height would you like to be?"

"Whatever height is best for the boys to kiss me," she said with a sly grin and a twinkle in her eye.

*"Want to know who I have a crush on?" a girl asked during the middle of her piano lesson. Before I could answer, she continued, "You know

that actor that plays Harry Potter?" At my nod, she went on, "He used to just be baby-cute, but now he's MAN-cute!"

*A middle school girl breezed into her lesson one afternoon and asked loudly, "So how's your boyfriend? Aren't you talking to someone?"

With a laugh, I said, "He's great. Why do you ask?"

"Oh, come on!" she urged. "You can tell me more. What happens at piano lessons stays at piano lessons!"

*An adorable seven-year-old boy with deep brown eyes stopped in the middle of his song, took his hands off the keys, and turned to me, "Do you know Kaley? In my class?"

"I don't know Kaley," I said. "Is she one of your friends?"

"Yeah," he nodded eagerly with a smile. "Well, I kinda love her," he said, his eyes lighting up. "I'm not sure if she loves me though, but just in case she doesn't, I have a backup plan."

"Really? What's your backup plan?"

"Annie!"

*"There's this boy in my class who likes me," a third-grade girl confided to me, "but I don't want to go out with him."

Laughing in my mind at what "going out" must mean to a third grader, I asked, "Why don't you want to go out with him?"

Wrinkling her nose, she said, "Because he spits a lot and sags his pants."

Take note, boys.

73

The White Easter

Tired and preoccupied, I was not prepared for Holy Week that year. I couldn't focus on this significant week in the church calendar.

It was the end of March. Spring was supposed to be starting, but the air was biting cold. And one day it snowed. "Snow," everyone kept saying, "in spring?" But when did one season ever instantly switch to another just because of the calendar?

One day at work that week, I glanced through a window to see large, whirling flakes pouring from the heavens, dancing above a barren earth. A wild beauty breathed peace to the turmoil that had been inside me that week.

Snow in spring. The earth rebelling. Didn't the earth also rebel on that fateful day of Jesus' death, when darkness covered the land, rocks split open, and the ground trembled violently?

Holy Week didn't arrive warm and sunny with birds cheerily singing the song of rebirth. It arrived with snow—pure, white, and clean—a fresh reminder to me of the meaning of the season. Jesus' agony in Gethsemane. Suffering and death on Good Friday. Triumphant resurrection.

"Though your sins are like scarlet, they shall be as white as snow." ~ Isaiah 1:18 (NLT)

Snow falling at Easter? Yes. It now seemed fitting.

One-line Prayers

What is that one bare-boned prayer you utter when you feel like you don't have any prayers left? What do you pray when you resign yourself to the fact that earthly healing isn't coming or that a certain dream won't come true? What is your one remaining, last-ditch prayer?

God, please help me.

Forgive me.

Why?

If not here, then someday in heaven . . .

I often come down to this simple prayer: "Help me to trust you with this."

Our fragmented and feeble one-line prayers can be so hard to pray. Just as we may withdraw from friends when life gets too overwhelming, we might also want to withdraw from God when no answer seems to be coming. But if God doesn't expect elaborately composed prayers from us when we are at our best, surely He doesn't expect them from us at our worst.

No matter how discouraged we are or how prayer-less, those single lines we offer up to heaven communicate just as much as beautiful, lengthy, hope-filled prayers. And, sometimes, those simple, one-line prayers might accomplish even more.

"The eyes of the Lord are toward the righteous and his ears toward their cry." ~ Psalm 34:15 (ESV)

Kids' Thoughts on My Fashion Sense

Many of my students, particularly the girls, catch on to how I enjoy putting outfits together and experimenting with accessories. It's easy for me to pick up on which little girls have that same interest when they admire my necklace and ask questions like, "Oooh, where did you get that?" "What is it made of?" "Did it come with that dress?"
Some of my girl students notice that I wear a small shoe size. One afternoon a pre-teen, home-school student declared, "When you get rid of those ankle boots, I want them!"

One other evening, a freckled fourth-grader gave me her completely truthful assessment of what I was wearing. After filling me in on her day at school, she glanced me over and said, "So, is there a reason you're all dressed up?"

"No reason," I answered. "I just enjoy being creative with outfits."

"Is that necklace Mother-of-Pearl?" she asked.

"Hmm, it's pearl, but I don't know about Mother-of-Pearl."

"How about your earrings? Are those real diamonds?"

"They came from the Cracker Barrel gift store, so probably not."

"Well, I love your boots! I've never seen any like that! They look kind of silly but cool at the same time. Like, the top half of your outfit looks all sweet and pretty, but the bottom half looks kind of wild and crazy, ya know?"

The Wordless Prayer

No whisper on my lips,
no murmur from my tongue.
Can you hear my prayer
when my heart has no words?

No answers for my mind,
no explanation why.
Can you hear me pleading
from so deep within?

No direction clear,
no peace, only fear.
Can you set my eyes
on what you plainly see?

No voice heard but doubt,
confused by its dark sound.
Can you speak louder
than my anxious mind?

I want to pour out words,
and know my voice is heard,
but can you hear me when
my heart just makes no sound?

"In the same way, the Spirit comes to help our weakness. We don't know what we should pray, but the Spirit himself pleads our case with unexpressed groans." ~ Romans 8:26 (CEB)

Even the Smallest Accomplishments

Post-performance week. I love this time.

This is the week students walk through my door after performing at the weekend's recital and, as their teacher, I get to celebrate their accomplishments with them or sympathize with their struggles.

I get to tell a girl that her performance held the audience spellbound. I get to tell a self-critical perfectionist that her performance was delightful, and would have been even if she hadn't performed flawlessly. I get to tell the boy, who had to skip his turn because he was sick in the bathroom with stage fright, that it is okay. "I used to get that nervous too. And there will be a next time. We will do this again and be successful." *Baby steps*, I think to myself and make a mental note: *Gradually acclimate him to playing in front of crowds. Build his confidence. Give him other, more comfortable opportunities to convince himself he can do it.*

I get to tell the girl who blundered her last recital, and had me sit with her on the piano bench for this one, that *she did it*. I don't mention that the rhythm was off. That doesn't matter right now. She had made that long walk to the stage, faced a large crowd, and played her piece from beginning to end. She thought she couldn't do it, but she proved to herself that she could.

The words I tell them aren't empty compliments or flattery, but truth. Sometimes I need to speak those words to myself when I'm discouraged with my own efforts.

We all have times when we are blind to our potential and need someone to pull the good out of us. When we are self-critical we need reminding that perfection is not required. When we are afraid to push through the uncomfortable stages of reaching our goals, we need to hear that others also faced that fear and discovered they were stronger than the challenge. Encouraging another person's fumbling attempts, coaxing someone past fear, or even celebrating someone's tiniest moments of progress might propel them further than they ever dreamed they could go.

A Thanksgiving Day Prayer

Dear God,

Every year when the
Thanksgiving season rolls
around, I recite my blessings
and recall the abundance you
pour into my life.

If I thanked you for every
single gift as it appeared, my
dialogue with you would have
no end, for you give so
generously in even the
simplest things. But
sometimes I fail to show my gratitude.

Perhaps I am preoccupied or too focused on life's trials, or maybe I have
grown spoiled by all your blessings and no longer notice them.
Sometimes, however, I simply fear.

I fear that if I delight in your bounty or rejoice in your provision, it will be
snatched away from me. The losses of life have taught me to fear being
too joyful and to be wary of hoping too deeply. I am sorry.

Remind me that fear does not come from you. Invite me to taste of your
goodness, cherish each blessing, and turn to you in lavish praise and
trustful thanksgiving.

Thank you for bringing even more good than I am able to see. Amen.

Kids' Thoughts on Technology

*"So, do you think you'll start practicing?" I asked an unmotivated boy for the hundredth time.

"I don't really like practicing at the piano," he said, biting his lip in thought. "But if there's some way I could practice on my phone. Maybe there's an app for that."

*Every week I write a practice goal in each student's notebook, recommending a minimum amount of total minutes that their practice should reach that week. One week, a cute girl with dainty freckles on her nose had exceeded her goal, and she wanted to make sure her extra practice minutes didn't go to waste. Her brown eyes widening, she asked eagerly,

"Do you offer rollover minutes?"

*"Hey!" a bubbly high school girl greeted me as she arrived at her lesson. "I'm so glad you finally joined Instagram—with all us younger people!"

To Be Bold

Sometimes I doubt my sacred worth.
Will I always fail and lose?
Although I feel the weight of doubt,
this I still can choose:
to be bold.

Sometimes I discount my own strength.
Do I have what it takes?
Yet even when I'm not convinced,
this choice I still can make:
to be bold.

Speech could falter, knees might shake,
and courage all rebel.
But stumbling over genuine words
does not mean I have failed
to be bold.

I might feel gripped and choked by fear,
afraid to lift my voice.
But timidity does not have the power
to rob me of my choice
to be bold.

More Than We've Asked For

"At Gibeon the Lord appeared to Solomon during the night in a dream, and God said, 'Ask me for whatever you want me to give you.'

"Solomon answered, 'Give your servant a discerning heart to govern your people and to distinguish between right and wrong. For who is able to govern this great people of yours?'

"The Lord was pleased that Solomon had asked for this. So God said to him, 'Since you have asked for this and not for long life, wealth for yourself, or the death of your enemies . . . I will do what you have asked. I will give you a wise and discerning heart, so that there will never have been anyone like you, nor will there ever be anyone like you. Moreover, I will give you what you have not asked for—both wealth and honor—so that in your lifetime you will have no equal among kings.'" ~ 1 Kings 3:5, 1 Kings 3:9-13 (NIV)

"God, please send the right students. Help with that unexpected bill. Then there's that medical test coming up." In my mid-twenties and living on my own for the first time, I'd begun the habit of writing down prayers on strips of paper and placing them in a small decorative, wooden box. Leaving my prayers in that box and shutting its lid symbolized letting go of my worries and trusting that God was at work.

Years later I still write out certain prayers and try to box up my worries with them. I kept those slips of papers with the original prayers and occasionally go back and read what I wrote as such a young woman. I'm astounded by how God has answered my prayers. Even more reassuring, I see how He has given me so much more than what I asked Him for.

In the book of First Kings, God asked Solomon in a dream what he would like to be given, and Solomon asked for wisdom to guide the people. In response, God declared that He would grant Solomon more wisdom than the world had ever seen; moreover, since Solomon hadn't asked for personal luxury, God promised to give that to Solomon also.

When I glance through those prayers that I wrote years ago, most of them sound very different from Solomon's prayer. Many of mine were personal requests for health, a prospering career, and the many other desires of my heart—and I do believe God wants to hear every concern and longing. Even though my pleas were not as noble or as eloquent as Solomon's, God still answered so many of them. But more than that, God supplied for many needs that never crossed my mind.

Eyes that can enjoy a sunset. A furry pet to snuggle. Hands that can draw, garden, or play musical instruments. Taste buds that enjoy a favorite meal. A friend who makes the day a little brighter. These are just some of a long list of gifts we perhaps never prayed for.

At times, though maybe not often enough, we pause to acknowledge the prayers God has answered. If we would also stop to recognize all He has given that we never prayed for, we would see how abundant and overwhelming His generosity truly is.

"Who among you will give your children a stone when they ask for bread? Or give them a snake when they ask for fish? If you who are evil know how to give good gifts to your children, how much more will your heavenly Father give good things to those who ask him." ~ Matthew 7:9-11 (CEB)

Kids' Thoughts on Gross Topics

* "Hey!" I greeted a small blond girl who had missed her last lesson. "Are you feeling better? I heard you've been pretty sick!"

With amusement in her eyes, she said, "When I threw up, you want to know what color it was?"

* A third-grade boy rushed into his after-school piano lesson, his face animated. "A boy barfed in class today!" he said. "I've seen someone barf in every single grade!" And then followed specific details.

*I pointed to a musical term on a teenage student's song and asked, "Do you know what 'cantabile' means?"

"Well," she said. "It looks sort of like 'cannibal,' sooo...."

*One evening I was teaching two sisters, when the older one announced, "I know what I want to be when I grow up. A masseuse! But I have two fears," she said as she made a face, "naked people and men with hairy backs."

*I was teaching a blond-headed boy and his little sister, who always read quietly in a book while her brother took his lesson. As I reminded her brother to count out his half notes, she approached me quietly and pointed to a phrase in the humorous children's book she was reading. "Ms. Misty, what do these two words mean?"

Since I've always loved vocabulary, I was eager to explain the words that had her confused. Her tiny finger pointed to these two words on the page: "bowel movement."

"Oh!" I said in surprise. "Those words mean, um, well, they mean..."

"Let me see!" her brother jumped in, grabbing the book from his sister's hands. "It says 'bowel movement,'" he announced, loud enough for the students and parents in the waiting area to hear.

"Yeah," she agreed, "but what is a bowel movement?"

"Maybe it's a misprint," her brother offered. "Maybe it's supposed to say 'vowel movement.' Maybe it's about consonants and vowels."

"No," she argued, raising her voice. "it says BOWEL MOVEMENT!"

"Shh!" I said as I noticed some heads in the waiting area turning our direction. "Bowel movement means, it means going to the bathroom."

"Going to the bathroom!" the two exploded into uncontrollable laughter.

When their mom arrived to pick them up, they rushed into the waiting area to greet her. They could have told her what they had learned in their lesson about half notes, quarter rests, or ledger lines. Instead, they blurted out what they thought was the most interesting tidbit of knowledge they had learned at their piano lessons. "Mom" they shrieked, "hey, Mom! Do you know what a BOWEL MOVEMENT is?"

*Gross topics also come up when I am babysitting. I sat at the kitchen table one evening drawing pictures with a little boy when he jumped up to run down the hall to the bathroom. When he returned, I said, "Hey, remember we're supposed to close the door when we use the bathroom, okay?"

"Oh, it doesn't bother me," he said plainly. "At school we have urinals, so I use the bathroom in front of people all the time."

"I know," I said, "but we also have to think about other people. To be polite and show manners to them, we need to shut the door when we're in the bathroom."

"But at school when I'm using the urinal, it doesn't bother the boys around me either. They don't care. We're all using the urinals."

"I know, buddy," I continued gently, "but this isn't a school with a big bathroom full of urinals. This is a house, with one bathroom that has a single toilet and a door that we close when we're using the bathroom."

He placed his chin in his hands and I could see his mind turning. *I think I've gotten through to him*, I thought.

"We've really gotta get some urinals in this house!" he finally said with a heavy sigh.

Purposely Flubbing a Spelling Bee

I squirmed with dread the afternoon Mrs. Meadows told our eighth-grade class to form a line in front of the chalkboard for the annual class spelling bee. Since reading, writing, and spelling were my favorite subjects, I had won quite a few spelling bees and competed in school and regional competitions. Success was expected. "Misty will win," students predicted as we trudged to the front of the classroom.

I wanted to disappear into the floor. *Just something else to feel pressured about,* I lamented to myself. Classmates and teachers had quickly caught on to my academic abilities, and I abhorred feeling expected to succeed in every subject. As a result, I didn't enjoy school much at all.

That eighth-grade year I made up my mind to not win that spelling bee. No way was I going to win a class spelling bee just to be handed a huge vocabulary study guide so that I could prepare for the school-wide competition. I already spent more than enough time on my homework load every night.

I stood against the blackboard in the line of middle schoolers. The students who had no interest in the spelling bee purposely flubbed up easy words on the first try, receiving looks of disapproval from Mrs. Meadows. How I wished I could do that! But the easy words came first. I couldn't pretend to miss them. Everyone would know if I bumbled an easy word on purpose. I had to be more strategic.

One by one, the line of students diminished as I waited longingly for a huge, horrible word, one I could blunder without it seeming intentional. Finally, the competition dwindled to just me and my classmate C.J., an intelligent, funny athlete who was well-liked by everyone. The class watched fascinated, as if viewing a hit movie where both of the main characters were protagonists but one would have to lose. "I don't know who to be for and who to be against," a few students whispered to each other. Who would win? The musical, academic girl who was painfully shy but greeted everyone with a smile? Or the smart athlete who was full of personality and involved in everything from football to the Student Council?

But no part of me wanted the pressure of carrying my class or school to the next match. *This is my moment*, I thought, my heart speeding up. *My decision.* I would go out with the so-called honor of runner-up, while escaping additional middle school pressures that were squeezing the life out of me already.

When another easy word came my way, I sighed softly and thought, *Please! Who doesn't know how to spell that? I can't blow a spelling bee on that word!* But then it came.

"Misty," Mrs. Meadows said. "Spell 'accommodate.'"

"Accommodate," I repeated and then thought silently, *two sets of double letters*. That would be an easy word to misspell. Slipping up on one of those double letters would be believable. "Accommodate," I said again.

I wasn't an actor, and I avoided the drama club, but I conjured up every facial expression I could muster, hoping to convince the class that I didn't know the word. "A-c-," I began, crinkling my eyes and putting on the best act I could, glancing thoughtfully around the room to stall for time. I breathed out another "c," looked down, and began wringing my hands.

"O," I continued, barely audible. *They're buying it!* I thought with relief. I gazed thoughtfully to the ceiling for a moment, my eyebrows creased, then whisked the remaining letters off my tongue: "m-o-d-a-t-e."

"That is incorrect," Mrs. Meadows responded. The class was full of sighs and "Oh!" said in unison, watching breathlessly to see if C.J. could pull off the correct letters.

Please. Please, get it. I inwardly begged him, wanting this whole game to be over. He slowly, methodically spelled the word: "A-c-c-o-m-m-o-d-a-t-e."

"That is correct," Mrs. Meadows said, and the class erupted in claps and cheers for the final two contestants. Always the gentleman even at such a young age, C.J. shook my hand as I smiled and congratulated him. I sat down at my desk, next to encouraging classmates who said, "Good job, Misty. That was a hard word. You got second place! Congrats!" But I just smiled back knowingly.

I watched as Mrs. Meadows handed C.J. a stack of study guides to prepare for the school-wide spelling bee and, with a snicker, I thought, *Sucker.*

I wasn't the one who'd be taking home a mountain of words to study. My after-school hours were already packed, trying to determine the value of *x* on endless algebra assignments.

Many people would not understand why I'd blown an opportunity to add another accomplishment to my school years. But, in the only way I was able to at the time, I was setting a limit and saying, "I can't take on any more." I think about this whenever I hear people say that they are appalled at the opportunity someone forfeited.

"Can you believe he didn't take that job? The pay was so much better!"
"Did you hear that she didn't accept that scholarship? What a waste!"
"He had an opportunity to transfer to a large city with more opportunities but kept his family in that little town instead!"

The thing is, we don't know the whole story. We don't know who is barely getting through the day. We don't know who is so overloaded that they can't take on any more responsibility. We don't know who might be dealing with deep struggles that take priority over whatever other opportunity lies in front of them. It's possible that what we think of as the best way ahead for someone might just add to their problems.

So the next time you wonder why someone didn't choose what you obviously thought was in their best interest, remember that exhausted young girl at the blackboard.

Kids' Thoughts on Holidays

*Most students aren't particularly excited when I suggest we turn on the metronome and nail down the rhythm with its clocklike ticks. One April, a middle school student entered my studio and announced, "I figured out what to give up for Lent! The metronome!"

*One evening at a group lesson, a student called out excitedly, "Ms. Misty, are we going to sing as a choir at our holiday recital?"

"Yes!" I answered. "I've been working on choosing some Christmas songs for us to sing this year, ones we haven't done yet!"

"Oh, I know, I know!" a student said as she bounced in excitement and shot her hand in the air.

"Yes?" I asked. "Do you have a song in mind for our choir to sing at the recital?"

"Yeah, I know a great one! Well, actually, I don't remember the name of the song, but I remember the band. They're called Daft Punk!"—an electronic dance disco band.

*I have some students who enjoy playing Christmas music all year long. One summer, a girl was doing excellent work on "Silent Night," when her little, six-year-old brother peered over her shoulder at the page and asked, "Did Jesus have a mohawk?"

I wasn't sure what he was talking about. Then I saw the book's simplistic, awkward looking halos drawn around the heads of the Holy Family. I kind of understood his confusion.

Would Jesus Flunk Algebra?

Fully God. Fully man.

When I reflect on the mysteries of this man—the son of God who chose to suffer on earth in human form—I'm in awe. Miraculously conceived by the Holy Spirit, sinless, and "one with the Father" (John 10:30), He

lived a human life of joy, pain, laughter, and disappointment. The mysteries of the incarnation flood my mind with questions and curiosity.

Did this Jesus—wisdom of God, who taught in the temple at the age of twelve—naturally do everything with perfection, or did He go through the awkward stages of learning that we go through? As Jesus learned carpentry from His father Joseph, did He ever hammer nails into uneven rows or build a wooden table with wobbly legs? Could His voice have drifted off-key while singing with His disciples at the Last Supper, or was the Savior of the world naturally gifted with perfect pitch? Did He bore people to sleep with His first sermons? Jesus preached and taught to thousands of people. Could someone have ever yawned and murmured to the man next to him, "That preacher should stick to carpentry"?

If He were in school today, would Jesus muddle through algebra class or need to use spell-check? If He was the most recent pro quarterback, would His team always reach the Super Bowl?

We may never know if Jesus had to be taught to count, or if he naturally read in all languages, or if he could draw a perfect replica of the Sea of Galilee. Despite all the mysteries about this man, this one thing He didn't keep secret from us:

He came to save us.

"The word became flesh and dwelt among us." ~ (John 1:14 NKJV).

God lived among us draped in human skin. He declared Himself to be "the way, the truth, and the life," our only route to the Father (John 14:6). Jesus revealed that He came to bring abundant life (John 10:10), and that those who know Him would know the Father (John 14:7).

Kids' Thoughts on Marriage

Students often ask me questions that begin, "Ms. Misty, someday if you get married…"

*A girl in her early teenage years asked, "Ms. Misty, someday if you get married, can I be a bridesmaid?"

*An eleven-year-old girl asked, "Miss Misty, if you ever get married and have kids, will they be related to me since I'm your student?"

*I have one young student who asks me every week if I've gotten married since the last time she saw me last, which would be the week before.

*A nine-year-old boy I was babysitting had some of his own thoughts on the subject. I was trying to encourage him to do some of his chores more independently. "Come on," I said. "You can do this! Keep trying! I live by myself, and I have to do a lot of things on my own too!"

"Why don't you get married?" he asked, shifting the conversation from his chores.

"Hmm." I tapped my finger against my face as I pretended to think about it. "Any ideas on how I could get married?"

I was surprised at how quickly he responded with what he thought was the perfect plan, "Go to a college place. Find a guy. You gotta like him, and he's gotta like you. Then, well, after that, I don't know how it works."

I'm not sure what I laughed at harder at—his statement of not knowing how it works "after that" or that he thought I was young enough to find a guy at a "college place."

*Another time, a seven-year-old asked, "Why don't you have a husband?"

"That's a good question," I replied. "Think you could help me find one?"

"I don't know where one is," he answered simply.

Me neither, kiddo. Me neither.

The Simplicity of Worship

When people hear the word "worship," certain images probably come to mind—perhaps a beautiful sanctuary with stained glass windows, contemporary praise music or old-time hymns, or heads bowed in prayer. We also tend to confine worship to a particular time or place, or attach it to elements like music, scripture, pastors, or priests.

Yet worship goes deeper than even the most beautiful, meaningful elements of a church service. It is an inner attitude, a focus and attentiveness on who or what matters most to us. Definitions of worship include words like "adoration" and "showing reverence to a deity." While that can definitely take place in the presence of scripture, preachers, or stained glass windows, it can also occur in places that look the least holy—jail cells, smoky rooms, chaotic factories, among endless piles of laundry or the simplest daily tasks.

Mary and Joseph worshiped in a filthy stable. Paul and Silas praised God behind prison walls. David danced in the streets. A grateful woman honored Jesus with perfume in the home of a leper.

Don't for a moment think that church is the only place where God can be worshiped. Anywhere we are, we can have an inner attitude of worship. Any place can become our sanctuary.

Always Lives

I found a copy of this poem I wrote when I was thirteen years old. It had been typed and printed in a church bulletin dated Easter 1991.

He must have come from heaven above to die on the cross for me.
He must have had a lot of love to lay down his life at Calvary.

He must have been the Son of God to know this was salvation's plan,
to let the men mock him and drive nails through his hands.

He must have been our loving Savior, our Savior Jesus Christ,
to turn to the thief on the cross and take him to paradise.

He must have cared a lot for us to show all the love He gives
by being raised from the dead to reassure us He always lives.

Rehearsing Mistakes

"If any of you lacks wisdom, let him ask God, who gives generously to all without reproach, and it will be given him." ~ James 1:5 (NASB)

From as early as I can remember, I had fallen in love with music and surrounded myself with it. As a little tot, I stood up at a VBS commencement night and sang, "Jesus called them one by one. Andrew, Peter, James, and John. They were fishing by the sea. Jesus said, 'Come foller me.' They'll foller Jesus, they'll foller Jesus."

I recall hurriedly putting on my pink dancing shoes whenever I would hear the first strains of "Girls Just Want to Have Fun" or sitting glued to the TV when "The Mandrell Sisters" came on. "I want to be like them when I grow up!" I declared excitedly.

When my parents enrolled me in piano lessons at age ten, I began building a more concrete foundation under my dreams. I spent hours practicing on an antique piano that didn't stay in tune, while my dad, never complaining, lay in front of the TV trying to hear his favorite shows.

When family, friends, and other adults heard I was taking piano lessons, they often tried to encourage me with the classic quote, "Practice makes perfect! Right?" And I would nod excitedly with a determined smile.

Fast forward several years. I became a piano teacher in my mid-twenties. As much as I loved music, I had never imagined that one day I would teach it. And of course, there's that general opinion held by some, that music can be an enjoyable hobby but not a successful career. I was surprised, therefore, to discover I could make music my full-time profession.

I was also surprised that I learned much more in a teacher's role than I did as a student. One such lesson was that the old adage "Practice makes perfect" wasn't necessarily true. Practice did not always make perfect, but it definitely "makes permanent."

Week after week, I would write specific instructions in students' notebooks about how to practice. *Count out half notes. Pause at the quarter rests. Correct measure fourteen of "Tulip Poplar."*

Despite sending my students home with detailed directions, many would go through the routine motion of practicing their songs without ever reading my instructions in their notebooks. They would return to lessons the following week, repeating the same mistakes they'd played the week before, with no changes or improvements whatsoever. Worse than that, not only did they replay their mistakes, but after a week of at-home practice, the mistakes were more deeply ingrained in their playing and even harder to correct.

This simple principle applies to so much more than learning a musical instrument. Whatever thoughts, words, or actions we repeat become long-lasting. Whether helpful or harmful, what we routinely practice becomes permanent.

Whether we rehearse thoughts that tell us we can reach our goal or thoughts that tell us we're doomed to fail, they become permanent. Whether we rehearse responses of shaking off irritations or letting them destroy our entire mood, they become our habitual responses. Whether we take continuous baby steps toward our goals or repeatedly talk ourselves into staying in our comfort zone, we are building consistent results. By repeating the same old thoughts or actions, we map be producing the same old mistakes.

Whenever we next hear the word "rehearse" or "practice," let's remember that it not only applies to musicians preparing for a show or athletes training for a game. Let's remember that we are daily rehearsing whom we will eventually become.

Woman at the Well

Weary from the road, Jesus paused at Jacob's well.
He sat to rest and catch His breath from the journey and the heat.
He saw her in the distance. He'd been waiting for her there.
She approached with hesitation, then He asked her for a drink.

"Sir, why do you ask me?" she responded in surprise.
"I'm a woman from Samaria, and are you not a Jew?
My people don't acknowledge yours;
your people don't acknowledge mine.
I should not speak to you."

With eyes that saw her wounded soul, Jesus continued to speak,
"My dear woman, if you only knew just whom you stand before,
if you knew this gift of God, you'd ask me for a drink.
I could give you Living Water, and you would thirst no more."

"Sir," the woman responded; her confusion He could tell,
"you have nothing to draw water with, and the well is deep.
Are you greater than our father Jacob, who gave us this very well?
Where is this Living Water of which you speak?"

Jesus answered the Samaritan woman, His voice soft and slow,
"The water you draw from this well shall leave you thirsty again.
But I give Living Water that shall rise and overflow,
and well into eternal life, with streams that never end."

Living Water that covers our sin and rids our souls of guilt,
Living Water that washes impurities until we are made clean.
Living Water that brings forgiveness and drowns all shame within.
And as He did for that Samaritan woman, He offers us a drink.

Living Water that consumes every fear and leaves peace in its wake,
LIving Water that soothes each wound and sets healing to begin.
Living Water that wipes out discouragement
and plants hope in its place.
And to each of us, Jesus invites, "Never thirst again."

Kids' Thoughts on Age

* "You know," I said to a middle-school girl who rarely touched the piano, "when I was young, I practiced for hours."

"Yeah," she snapped, "but that was in the old days."

* I'm amused by how easily students confuse different people who were literally born in "the old days."

"Did you and your sister get those new piano books?" I asked a sixth-grade girl.

"Yeah," she said, "my sister got one with Albert Einstein on the front of it."

"Albert Einstein?" I asked in confusion.

"Or Beethoven."

* One day I accidentally asked a spunky, strawberry-blond girl the same music question twice. "You already asked me that! Don't you remember?" she blurted out.

"Oh, it's just that old brain of mine," I said. "It forgets easily. Have I just gotten too old to be a teacher?"

At her quick and firm "Yes," I said, "What? Are you serious! At what age should grown-ups quit teaching?"

"At thirty-nine," she said.

"Thirty-nine! But that's still pretty young to quit teaching, isn't it?"

"Nope! It's not!" she shook her head.

"So you're saying that after thirty-nine a teacher should just throw in the towel and give up, right?"

"Yes!" she declared. "They should just quit!" She waved her arm dramatically in the air. "Hire somebody else!"

*"Did you know," a feisty seven-year-old girl began, "that older girls go out dancing in crop tops? In tops that show their belly buttons?"

"Well, I'm an older girl, and I don't go out dancing in crop tops," I countered.

"Not old like you! Your crop top would rip!"

*A sixth-grade girl told me at her first lesson, "I don't like a lot of the newer songs. I'm more interested in older music."

"Me too!" I answered excitedly, not hearing this comment often from students her age. Lyrics I grew up with in the 1980s and 90s began floating through my mind as I asked, "What era of music do you like?"

"Songs from the early 2000s," she said. I was older than I realized.

*Often students or parents are surprised to discover I'm not younger than I am. I remember the day a middle-school student repeatedly asked how old I was, until I finally gave in and told her.

"Okay, okay, I'm thirty-seven," I told her.

"What?!" Her eyes bugging out, she argued, "No, you're not!"

"I am," I laughed, "although I'm very flattered. Let's get on to your song though."

A couple of weeks later, she confided that she hadn't believed me, so she went home and told her mom, who said that I must be playing an April Fool's prank on them—until her mom turned to Google to discover that I was telling the truth.

*Not all kids I work with consider me as young as that girl did. One day a boy asked me, as he was updating information in his phone, "When was your birthday?"

"January 13th," I answered.

"January 13, what year?" he asked.

"1978," I answered.

"1978? Whoa!"

"Long time ago, huh?"

"Really long time ago."

"You think we had cars back then?"

"Probably not."

*One boy at his piano lesson referred to me as "one of those sweet, little old ladies who teaches piano." Another said he thinks of people like me as "age-enhanced."

On the days I leave work after teaching kids who are loaded up on sugar from a school party or after a student claims that, after months of lessons, I never once taught her Middle C, I most definitely do feel "age-enhanced."

This Gift of Time

All we have is this moment now to gaze above and wonder how
our God knows each star by name and shines moonlight in the dark.

All we have is this moment now to take our brokenness and bow
before the One who heals our pain and mends our broken heart.

All we have is this moment now to enjoy the gifts our God endows,
to feel the sun, to dance through rain, to see beauty near and far.

All we have is this moment now to lift a soul who feels cast down,
to offer love without restraint, despite our wounds and scars.

This moment will pass swiftly by. Don't take for granted this gift of time.
The person whom you choose to be could change someone's eternity.

Zechariah's Story

A faithful Judean couple,
side by side, growing old,
had served the Lord for many long years,
without a baby to hold.

Zechariah entered the temple,
where he steadfastly served the Lord.
While burning incense at the altar,
a holy voice he heard.

"Don't be afraid, Zechariah,"
spoke an angel of God.
"Your prayer has been heard, your wife will conceive,
and you will name the boy John.

He will bring joy to many,
filled with God's Spirit before even born.
He'll turn the people's hearts toward God
and prepare the way of the Lord."

Zechariah asked, "How can I be sure?
My wife and I have grown old."
The angel answered, "Since you don't believe,
your voice shall not utter a word."

Zechariah rushed out of the temple
to those awaiting his return.
He gestured with trembling hands
that he'd seen an angel of the Lord.

Zechariah returned home in silence;
his wife Elizabeth became with child.
Her heart was filled with gratefulness
for on her barrenness God had smiled.

Time swiftly passed, the months flew by,
and Elizabeth's labor began.
"His name will be John," the couple declared,
and Zechariah could speak once again.

John grew and matured in spirit
and just like the angel's words,
he urged the people to turn to God
and prepared the way of the Lord.

Little Girls Learning Metaphors

 I walked into my studio on a Wednesday after lunch. Along with teaching piano that afternoon, I would be tutoring two girls with their schoolwork. I had known the two girls, ages nine and eleven, and their family for a few years. With fair hair, big eyes, and sweet voices that loved to sing, the girls were impossible not to adore.

Their school lesson that day was on similes and metaphors. I had always loved writing and studying the English language, but Lucy and Jenny didn't find it as fascinating as I did. After explaining how similes make comparisons using the words "like" or "as," and how metaphors make comparisons by saying that one thing is something else, I set the girls to writing sentences with examples of each.

"Okay," I said to the younger of the two. "You first, Lucy. What sentence did you come up with to give an example of a metaphor?"

Her large hazel eyes looked at her paper as she read aloud, "Jack is a small boy," referring to her little brother.

"Well," I began, "that's actually not a metaphor because Jack really is a small boy. To make it a metaphor, we would have to say that Jack is something he really isn't. Like," I thought for a moment, "does Jack ever get wild and crazy and like to run and climb on things?" At her enthusiastic nod, I said, "So you could say something like, 'Jack is a wild monkey,' and that would be a metaphor."

Lucy's eyes lit up, "Okay, I'll write, 'Jack is a wild, funny monkey.'"

I then turned to her sister. "Okay, Jenny, what metaphor did you come up with?"

Smiling her trademark smile, she read, "Jenny is a talented artist." Realizing I must not have explained myself very well, I said, "Well, that's actually not a metaphor because it's true. You are a talented artist. But we could turn it into a metaphor by saying something like, 'Jenny is a regular Michaelangelo.'"

"Who's Michaelangelo?" both girls piped up.

"Who's Michaelangelo? He's an Italian artist who painted the Sistine Chapel! Here," I said, reaching for my ipad to make a quick Google search. "Look at this. Michaelangelo painted all this on the ceiling of the Sistine Chapel. Look at all the detail. Can you imagine one person painting all that by hand!"

Jenny took my ipad and immediately zoomed in on the figures. "WHOA. Those men he painted are really muscular—and naked."

"Let me see!" Lucy piped up and hurried to join her sister.

"Hey," I jumped in, wondering how we'd gone from metaphors to naked, muscular men. I reached for my ipad and quickly googled Painting of the Last Supper. "Let's switch to Leonardo da Vinci!"

120

Psalm 23

He guides and cares for His children who stumble.
In Him I have all that I need.
He invites me to rest in the peace of His presence,
where He restores and comforts me.

He leads me to live in the truth that He teaches,
the wisdom of all His ways.
He stays ever with me and quiets my fears
on the darkest and most daunting days.

He blesses and loves me when others despise.
His abundance surpasses my need.
His mercy and goodness will last all my life
and remain through eternity.

Kids' Thoughts on Performing

Throughout the year I offer various opportunities for my students to perform. I'm always intrigued by the different personalities that emerge from students as we prepare for those events. Some kids get excited about their time to shine; others are terrified. Others seem completely indifferent to whether they will perform well; they might even arrive at the recital completely unprepared.

I remember a second-grade girl who was so intense about her upcoming recital that I emphasized only the fun and enjoyment of it. "The recital is gonna be so fun, Marlee! I want you to enjoy it and have a good time. If you hit a wrong note, just keep going. No big deal."

"It is a big deal!" she bawled and threw her head and arms down on the piano keys, which resulted in a startling crashing of notes that reflected her mood. "I can't hit one wrong note. Not a single one! I've got to get it just perfect! This is a once-in-a-lifetime opportunity!" she wailed.

Occasionally, students meet the challenge with so much confidence that they seem immune to stage fright. A little boy asked if he could play a song from under the piano at the recital. One adult beginner student was so motivated that she wanted to have a live band back her up.

I've also taught students who are more than eager for their time in the spotlight. "Isn't this your first recital with me?" I asked a sassy little girl with strawberry blond hair. "It'll go like this. You will sit with your family, and when I call your name you'll come up to the piano and play your songs."

"Make sure you give the audience time to clap for me," she said.

Many of my students are not as bold as that little girl, and they will definitely let me know of their uncertainties. I once tried every way possible to talk a little boy into singing with the other students at our recital. He was terrified of having to perform in front of an audience of seventy-five.

"I'm not good at performing in front of fifteen thousand people!" he said. "Who do you think I am? Bruno Mars?"

That Little Town of Bethlehem

"And his name shall be called Wonderful, Counselor, The Mighty God, The Everlasting Father, The Prince of Peace." ~ Isaiah 9:6 (KJV)

I can still remember the song's gentle melody as the children in my hometown church presented the yearly nativity play—shy voices singing as the narrator paused to allow shepherds adorned in bathrobes to make their entrance.

"O little town of Bethlehem, how still we see thee lie. Above thy deep and dreamless sleep, the silent stars go by..."

As we sang those words, I pictured a sleepy Bethlehem village holding the secret of a newborn king, its inhabitants dreaming blissfully, unaware that this night was any different from the other nights. Many years later, one of those familiar lines hit me in a way it never had:

"The hopes and fears of all the years are met in thee tonight."

People who traveled those Bethlehem roads two thousand years ago, and people walking roads today, felt the crippling pangs of fear or the disappointment of unfulfilled hopes. The yearning for a rescuer to enter into and lift their heavy weight of brokenness may have seemed too good to be true.

Yet when Jesus slipped quietly to earth through Mary's womb, He came as the Savior, the One who desired to meet every person amid whatever hopes and fears had long churned within each soul. This Comforter came into this earthly existence as a tiny weak infant—as helpless as we may feel—yet offering peace for trembling hearts and hope for relentless disappointments.

The night angelic choirs visited a few shepherds and a certain star caught the attention of some Wise Men, most of Bethlehem had no idea the world had changed radically. The Everlasting Light arrived so quietly, easily overlooked in the darkness. He arrived in the simplest way—just another baby born in a small town to meager parents.

Likewise, when we feel lost on the road and weary, we usually don't experience ethereal voices or a shining light that directs us to God's doorsteps.

Jesus may not come to us with a jubilant chorus of angels.

But He comes.

He may not come to us with a dynamic spotlight pointing out the path we need to take.

But He comes.

He usually comes softly, gradually, wrapped in such simplicity that we easily overlook Him.

But He comes.

When we feel consumed by brokenness and weariness, Jesus comes. He sits right down in the middle of our long-held hopes and deep heart-rending fears. Indeed, "the hopes and fears of all the years are met in thee tonight."

Into the Wilderness

Into the wilderness Jesus went.
By the Spirit He had been sent,
so Jesus stayed.

.

There in the desert fasting,
His suffering long-lasting,
Jesus prayed.

Hungry, weak, exhausted,
alone there with His Father,
Jesus heard

the tempter raise his head
and command, "Turn this stone to bread."
Jesus spoke God's Word.

"Man lives not by bread alone,
but by each word the Father spoke."
Still Satan tried,

"Each kingdom that you see,
can be yours. Just worship me!"
Jesus replied,

"The Father made it known
to worship Him and Him alone,"
Then Satan led

Jesus to the height,
of the holy worship site.
The tempter said,

"Cast yourself from here!
you know your angels will appear,
if you're God's Son!"

Jesus answered, "My Father says
not to tempt Him nor to test."
Then Satan was gone.

Angels rushed to our Lord's side
to strengthen, to provide
for His needs.

In spite of weakness, hunger, and thirst,
Jesus showed us that at God's word
Satan must flee.

Celebrating the Prince of Peace

"Peace I leave with you, My peace I give to you; not as the world gives do I give to you. Let not your heart be troubled, neither let it be afraid." ~ John 14:27 (NKJV)

Every year, after the hours of Thanksgiving had passed, I would excitedly beg my parents to bring the Christmas tree down from the attic. Soon my brother and I were untangling lights and digging through boxes of handmade ornaments.

After the tree was up, my parents would have to drag me to bed that night because I was determined to sleep under the tree. I loved lying there, gazing up at its web of sparkling colors. In the quiet darkness, those twinkling lights washed a sense of peace over me. Despite my childish worries or the fears I felt from overhearing snippets of news reports, I knew that a baby long ago born into a poor family had come to rescue the world. And as I would gaze into lights reflecting off glass angels and silver stars, I knew this also: He had come to rescue me.

A dark room lit only by the warmth of Christmas lights still soothes and calms my soul. The gentle glow whispers to me that the Prince of Peace descended to this messy, broken world to offer us peace that passes all understanding.

"You keep him in perfect peace whose mind is stayed on you, because he trusts in you." ~ Isaiah 26:3 (ESV)

For Teens & Youth

Through years of working with kids and teenagers, I get many opportunities to see life through their eyes and understand their struggles. *Devozine* magazine for teens and youth has published many of my devotionals. I dedicate these next four pieces to the young people I've worked with and all those making their way through that season of life.

When We've Forgotten How to Smile

"God cares for you, so turn all your worries over to Him." ~ 1 Peter 5:7 (CEV)

"You have a really beautiful smile— when you do smile." I read those words written in the back of my freshman yearbook as classmates cheerfully passed around the new publications for signatures. Those last few words nagged at me so much that I contemplated scratching them out. *Me?* I thought in quiet surprise. *I don't smile much? But in elementary school, I was always referred to as the shy, sweet girl who was always smiling. Have I lost that?* I wondered.

As I finished my freshman year of high school, I wasn't smiling much. Striving to keep up with the pressures of school and the perfectionistic demands I'd placed on myself had left me carrying a heavy emotional weight. Reading those words in my yearbook, I felt disappointed for letting that season of my life steal so much of my joy.

If I could go back to my high school years, I wouldn't seek perfection or others' approval. I would try to make positive, healthy decisions and be proud of my efforts. I would smile confidently and remember that God never designed human shoulders to carry the weight of the world. I might have remembered to look up away from my stresses from time to time and smile more smiles. Then maybe the comment in my yearbook would have simply read, "You have a really beautiful smile."

My Father Says

"And even the very hairs of your head are all numbered. So don't be afraid; you are worth more than many sparrows."
~ Matthew 10:30-31 (MEV)

You might think I'm unworthy and less than I should be,
but my Father says I'm valued, so I affirm, "Yes, this is me."

Others might not want me or reject the traits I bring,
but my Father says I'm chosen, so I declare, "This is me."

I might not be too popular or the leader of the team,
but my Father says I matter, so I answer, "This is me."

I might feel insufficient and not like the self I see,
but my Father says I'm His, so I proclaim, "This is me."

It Can Get Better

"Someday you're going to wish you were back." Those were the words well-meaning adults often responded with after they'd asked how I liked school and I gave them my honest answer. I have some bright, cheerful memories of particular grades in elementary school and the time spent with friends there. Middle and high school, however, were completely different stories.

Each year when August rolls around, I greet my piano students eager to hear about their first few days of school. Some are happy to have a daily place to socialize again; others are glum that carefree summer days are over. All are exhausted.

The words I'm careful to never say are, "Someday, you're going to wish you were back."

The truth is, as much as I enjoy catching up with classmates online and bumping into them in the community, I have never wished I could go back to my school years. I am happy in my career and the opportunities it gives me to be creative. I love finding ways to share what I believe are the gifts I am meant to share with the world. But I have never wished I could go back to the days of wagging around a backpack too heavy for my eighty-pound frame, wondering where to sit in the lunchroom where everyone subdivides into their own little groups, or studying way past the time I should be in bed.

So I don't try to paint students' time in school as a glorified season and that life will only go downhill once those days are over. Hopefully, they will look back on their time in school with pleasant memories. But some of them might need to be reminded of what I learned only after that young season of life was over: it can get better.

For Teens & Youth

Hope for Tomorrow

"Therefore do not worry about tomorrow., for tomorrow will worry about itself. Each day has enough trouble of its own." ~ Matthew 6:34 (NIV)

At some point in life, most of us go through seasons where we lose all feelings of hope for tomorrow. After being deeply let down or repeatedly dealing with disappointment, trying to unearth a sense of hopefulness can seem impossible. Where we might have once tried to face the future with optimism, fear often takes its place—fear of what blow is coming next, fear of what seam in our life could be unraveling at this very moment, fear of enjoying happy moments because we've learned to keep our guard up.

I've had times in life when I quit looking forward to what was ahead. With my future appearing barren and defeated, at least to my earthly eyes, I simply tried to endure each day. I thought I was being cautious and wise, yet I was actually reinforcing fear as I practiced expecting the worst.

I still have moments when fear threatens to steal my joy and peace, and I have plenty of times I catch myself anticipating the worst-case scenario. I often must remind myself that God's desire for me is to live in daily assurance, enjoying the countless gifts He gives and trusting Him to provide for any needs tomorrow, in even the biggest and simplest things.

Quiet Joy

I sat on the second pew in the sanctuary to get a clear view of the choir as they performed their Christmas cantata. Lights shone on Christmas wreaths, and two small girls wriggled in the pew beside me.

The first song began, slow and tender, with the added harmony of a violin and cello. Throughout the gentle piece, voices soothingly repeated the melodic phrase, "How Great Our Joy."

I usually associate songs about joy with an upbeat tempo and a driving beat—loud drums, a moving bass line, a jubilant melody. But the song progressed, slowly and delicately, without flash or accelerando. I loved the contrast. I loved the metaphor.

Like that song, joy isn't always dramatic. It isn't always fireworks flashing or bubbling laughter or a glittering gift. Joy doesn't always shout. It might come as a whisper in the ordinariness of our lives. Sometimes joy is quiet and calm, like rising from bed and welcoming the morning, despite the disappointments of yesterday.

Yes, joy awaits us—
in even the simplest things.

I'm a native of Smiths Grove, Kentucky, where I live in the countryside about five miles from my little hometown. My lifelong passions have always been writing and music. You can often find me typing out stories on my chromebook or practicing for my next musical performance. My regular work consists of teaching piano lessons on a full-time basis and working with kids in a side job or two. In my spare time, I'm often outside my house enjoying my four acres of nature.

Thank you for reading my second book, *In The Simplest Things*. If you missed my first one, look up *Finally Spoken: Words of Hope*. Both are available on Amazon. You can also connect with me at www.facebook.com/StudioOfMistyLButler or email me at StudioOfMistyLButler@gmail.com.

Thanks again for letting me share my writing with you!

Sincerely,
Misty

Made in the USA
Lexington, KY
29 October 2019